solos *for* guitar

by Ed Lozano

The fun and simple way to learn the basics of lead guitar while playing with a band. Special sections on scales and arpeggios, playing over changes, how to create a solo, and much more.

Cover photograph of Gibson ES-335 by Randall Wallace
courtesy of The Wallace Collection
Author photograph by Scott Abrams
Project editor: Ed Lozano
Interior design and layout: WR Music Service

Order No. AM 971443
US International Standard Book Number: 0.8256.1902.5
UK International Standard Book Number: 0.7119.8980.X

Exclusive Distributors:
Music Sales Corporation
257 Park Avenue South, New York, NY 10010 USA
Music Sales Limited
8/9 Frith Street, London W1D 3JB England
Music Sales Pty. Limited
120 Rothschild Street, Rosebery, Sydney, NSW 2018, Australia

Printed in the United States of America by
Vicks Lithograph and Printing Corporation

Amsco Publications
New York/London/Paris/Sydney/Copenhagen/Madrid

CD Track Listing

Contents

Acknowledgements

I would like to thank:
- Peter Pickow and Dan Earley whose patience, knowledge, and guidance proved invaluable; without their help this book would not have been possible.
- All of the folks at Music Sales Corp.
- My family and friends (you know who you are)
- The countless number of blues musicians whose recordings have been an education and inspiration.
- And finally, to the Creator for all of the above and then some. I humbly gassho before you.

Preface

The blues is an American artform that dates back to the early 1900s. This music style was born out of the desire for true freedom of expression. The themes expressed in this musical style are basic human qualities that people from all walks of life can identify with. The blues is about expressing those basic human emotions that are inside all of us. From the pain of love lost to the joy of love found, from traveling endlessly to finding your way home, "The blues is simply. . . ," as Willie Dixon so eloquently and succinctly put it, ". . . the facts of life."

Every musical genre, from jazz to country to rock and soul, has a direct lineage to the blues. Heavy metal and hip-hop are not immune to the infectious grooves and shuffles while R&B and swing draw directly from its well.

The blues is simple to understand and with a little bit of practice you can begin to master the subtleties that make this music so much fun.

So—whether you're looking to rock, honky-tonk, groove, swing, jam, *etc.*—learning the blues can help you to better express yourself.

① Introduction

Welcome to *Easy Blues Solos for Guitar*!

This instruction method has been tried and tested with many students. Some have gone on to play professionally while others have enjoyed the ability to express themselves in front of a few friends and family while still others have simply just entertained themselves.

The music examples are graded beginning with basic rhythms and rests, to scales and arpeggios, to playing over chord changes, and progressing to more challenging techniques. These examples are clearly demonstrated on the accompanying CD with each scale and arpeggio practiced over one chord. The CD also includes a backup (or practice track) for you to play along with. All of the examples are then demonstrated over two- and three-chord progressions.

There is also a section covering intros, turnarounds, and endings. Next, the method continues with a discussion on improvising that describes how to create a solo using some advanced techniques. Finally, the last section has five solos demonstrating the techniques that you've learned in a variety of styles.

This method is set up to take the student from basic ideas that are applicable in real-life playing situations to actual licks and riffs that make up the blues vocabulary.

Easy Blues Solos for Guitar, when used in conjunction with *Easy Blues Rhythms for Guitar*, provides the most comprehensive blues method for the beginning guitarist. Additionally, both of these books provide a preparatory for the *Easy Blues Songbook* which puts together all of the tools necessary for the guitarist that is ready to proceed to the next level; that is, forming a band, making a set list, *etc.*

If the blues have found you then the *Easy Blues Method* will help you find your voice to truly express yourself.

Basic Tablature and Standard Notation

The music in this book has been written in both guitar *tablature* and standard notation. The tablature system has had a long history dating back to the lute music of the Renaissance. Today's TAB system uses six horizontal lines; each line represents a string of the guitar, with string 1 being the highest and string 6 the lowest. The numbers that appear on our TAB staff indicate the fret position, while a zero indicates that the string should be played open.

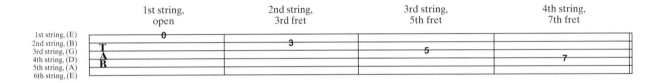

Tablature will only give you the pitch—you have to look at the standard notation to determine the duration of each note. Refer to the chart below for a breakdown of note values.

Chord and Scale Frames

The frames used to illustrate chords and scales are fairly easy to read. The frame depicts a portion of the guitar's fretboard. The vertical lines represent the strings of the guitar with the thickest string to the left and the thinnest to the right. The horizontal lines represent the frets. The nut of the guitar is represented by the bold horizontal line at the top of the diagram. If the top line is not bold then the frame represents a section of the middle of the fretboard with the exact location indicated by the fret number to the right of the frame. The dots that appear in the frames illustrate where you should place your fingers. An **X** above the top line indicates that that string should be muted or not played while an **O** above the top line indicates that that string should be played open.

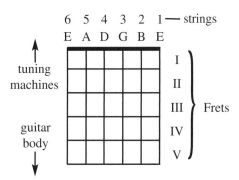

How to Use This Book

The purpose of this book/CD method is to teach you about basic blues lead guitar playing. All of the examples are played with a backing band and there is a backup track for you to play along. The backup track has a rhythm guitar, bass guitar, and drums. These tracks provide you with the opportunity to practice in a "live" atmosphere.

Q: How do you learn how to play with a band without playing with a band?
A: By practicing with a band. Even the beginner examples are recorded with a band so you'll be learning how to play in a live situation right from the start.

Listen to the CD and follow along with your book. You can then practice with the example as it's playing or practice with the backup track provided at the end of each section. Each example has a count off so that you'll know when to start playing. Set the backup track to repeat and play for as long as you like. Either way you'll be learning as you play and playing as you learn.

The techniques outlined in this book are the basics of blues vocabulary. The ideas progress gradually. As you learn a new example you're reinforcing ideas and techniques that you had previously learned.

Music store racks are filled with riff and lick books as well as transcriptions of your favorite players. The question that you might ask yourself is "how do I get from playing a riff from a book to sounding like my favorite guitar player?" Well, this method will show how easy it is to take a scale, arpeggio, lick, or riff and play that musical phrase over each chord. Eventually that phrase will become part of your vocabulary.

I devised this method when I was first learning how to play. The first thing that I did was to play a rhythm guitar part with a metronome and then record that to a cassette deck. Needless to say, the backup tracks sounded rather boring. Later on I graduated to a four-track recorder and a drum machine. Finally, I had developed the technique and confidence to play with other musicians and attend open blues jams.

The following section, "Crash Course on Music Theory," takes you through all of the musical jargon necessary to fully understand the topics covered in this book and to communicate with other musicians. Those of you who are familiar with these concepts may wish to briefly scan the section while others new to music should study the section thoroughly.

All of the examples are in the key of A. A was chosen because it falls comfortably in the middle of the guitar neck. However, to fully understand the concept of improvising and develop good technique you should practice the scales and arpeggios in all twelve keys.

Crash Course on Music Theory

Some of you may be new to music, so before going any further let's discuss some basics. Music is a language and the better you understand the fundamental concepts of the language, the better you can communicate.

First, let's look at the musical alphabet. The staff below illustrates the notes available on the guitar.

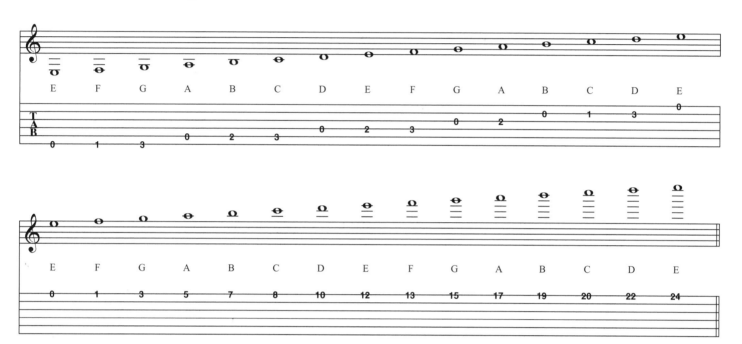

Notice that the letters that make up the note names repeat after every seven notes. The lowest note is an E which moves up to F and then up to G. At this point we go up again to the next note, which is A and the notes that ascend from this point on go up alphabetically from A to G. This cycle repeats itself until we run out of notes on the guitar.

Scales

The notes move up in a series of steps to form a *scale*. A *whole step* is the distance between two notes that are two frets apart, and a *half step* is the distance between any two adjacent notes. Take a look at the following example and notice that as the notes on the musical staff go up, so do the numbers on the tablature staff.

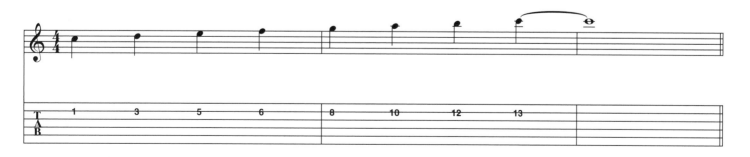

By changing the combination of whole steps and half steps we can change the scale type. We'll use the C major scale as our reference point. The chart below illustrates the scale with whole numbers and Roman numerals.

1	2	3	4	5	6	7	8
I	II	III	IV	V	VI	VII	VIII

The regular whole numbers refer to the *scale degrees*, or the notes themselves; for example, in the key of C major, scale degree 2 refers to the D note, scale degree 5 refers to the G note, scale degree 7 refers to the B note, *etc.* The distance between two notes, or one scale degree to another, is called an *interval*. The Roman numerals refer to chords.

Chords

A *chord* is made up of two or more notes played simultaneously. For example, a *C major triad* is made up of three notes; those three notes are scale degrees 1, 3, and 5—or notes C, E, and G.

Arpeggios

An *arpeggio* is simply a chord that has been broken into single notes.

Power Chords and Diads

Power chords and *diads* are two-note chords used in blues and rock. The ones that we'll be dealing with are fifth, sixth, and seventh chords. For instance, a C5 diad is made up of scale degrees 1 and 5 (or notes C and G). A C6 diad is made up of scale degrees 1 and 6 (or notes C and A). A C7 diad is made up of scale degrees 1 and $\flat$7 (or notes C and B$\flat$). These chord types are important for playing shuffle rhythms.

Progressions

A *progression* is a chord sequence or pattern. Just like two or more notes make up a chord, two or more chords make up a progression. In blues music a progression is commonly made up of chords I, IV, and V. In the key of C these chords would be C, F, and G. In this book most of the examples are in the key of A. The I, IV, and V chords in the key of A are A, D, and E.

Chord Charts and Leadsheets

Take a look at the diagram below.

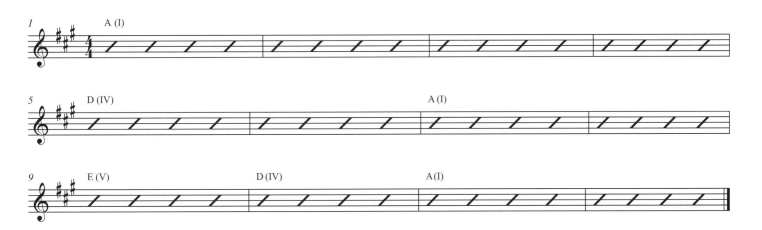

This is called a *chord chart*. It is very important to learn how to read these charts as they can guide you rather painlessly through an entire tune. Although this is just a basic twelve-bar blues progression, the chart helps you visualize what you should be playing.

The following chart contains some more complex notation but don't let that intimidate you.

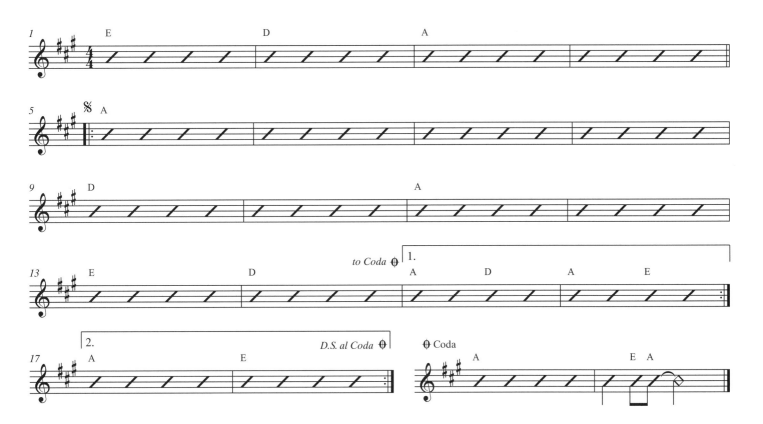

Now, let's go through the chart one step at a time:
- The *intro* consists of the first four *measures* or *bars*.
- The repeat sign (‖:) tells us that this is the measure that we repeat from when we reach this other repeat sign (:‖).
- Notice the twelve measures between repeat signs. This section is called the *verse* or *chorus*. In blues, these terms are interchangeable.
- The rhythm slashes that appear in each measure indicate that a rhythm pattern is being played but does not indicate a specific rhythm.
- The *first* and *second endings* indicate which ending to take depending on how many times you've played the section.
- The last two bars in a twelve-bar blues verse are often referred to as the turnaround. The *turnaround* is a descending (or ascending) pattern played at the end of a blues verse that brings you back to the top.
- The *segno* is the symbol (𝄋). *D.S. al Coda⊕ (Dal Segno al Coda)* indicates that you go back to the 𝄋, replay the section and then to the Coda (⊕).
- This symbol (‖) indicates the end of the tune.

A *leadsheet* is basically the same as a chord chart except that it includes the melody and the lyrics of the tune.

Before we begin playing, please refer to the "Tuning Track" on the CD and tune up. You may use an electronic tuner as all of the examples have been tuned to A=440.

Let's learn how to play the blues. . .

Part I: Basic Rhythms and Rests

Read the "Basic Tablature and Standard Notation" section to familiarize yourself with note values.

Each example is nine measures in length. You'll notice that there is a count off at the beginning letting you know when to start playing.

Learning how to play and count at the same time is very important. You may want to practice clapping the rhythms while you count out loud before you play the exercise. The bold numbers indicate when to play (or clap).

Whole Notes

One whole note equals four beats. Listen to the "count off" and prepare yourself to play on the 1 count and let the note ring for counts 2, 3, and 4. Count to yourself, "**1**, 2, 3, 4, **1**, 2, 3, 4, *etc.*" Notice that the one is emphasized. Play on the bold count.

Example 1

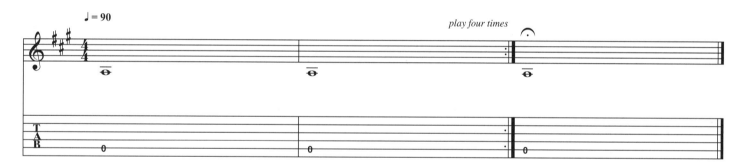

Half Notes

One half note equals two beats. The same basic idea that we just discussed in the previous example still applies. The difference is that you will now be playing on counts 1 and 3. Count to yourself, "**1**, 2, **3**, 4, **1**, 2, **3**, 4, *etc.*"

Example 2

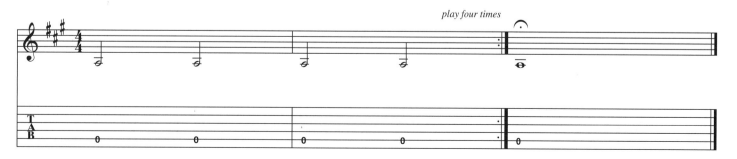

Quarter Notes

One quarter note equals one beat. Here we play on every beat. Count to yourself, "**1, 2, 3, 4, 1, 2, 3, 4,** *etc.*"

 Example 3

Eighth Notes

In this example there are two notes to every beat (or count). Here we play on and in between the beats. Count to yourself, "**1 & 2 & 3 & 4 & 1 & 2 & 3 & 4 &,** *etc.*"

 Example 4

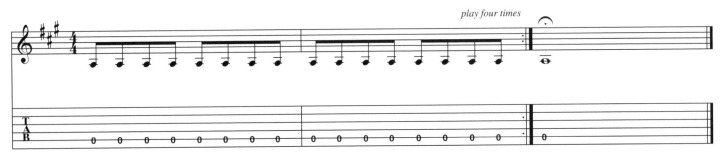

Whole Notes and Whole Rests

Learning how to play the rests is just as important as learning how to play the notes. Play the note and let it ring for 4 beats then use your fret hand to dampen (or mute) the string by lightly touching it just enough to keep it from ringing. Count to yourself, "**Play, 2, 3, 4, Mute, 2, 3, 4,** *etc.*"

 Example 5

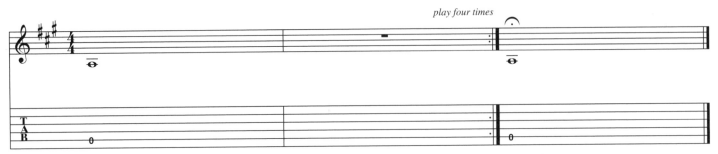

Half Notes and Half Rests

Now try playing for 2 beats and muting for 2 beats. Count to yourself, "**Play**, 2, **Mute**, 4, **Play**, 2, **Mute**, 4, *etc.*"

Example 6

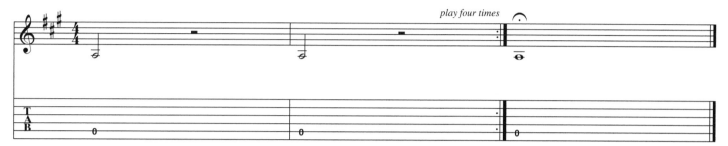

Quarter Notes and Quarter Rests

Play for 1 beat and mute for 1 beat. Count to yourself, "**Play**, **Mute**, **Play**, **Mute**, **Play**, **Mute**, **Play**, **Mute**, *etc.*"

Example 7

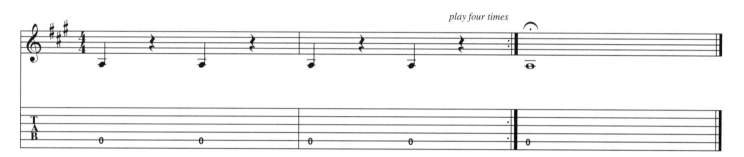

The "Charleston" Rhythm

This exercise is a little tricky as it has a dotted quarter note and eighth note tied to a half note pattern. It sounds more complicated than it actually is, just listen to the CD and I'm sure that you'll get it. Try counting a steady eighth-note pattern to yourself, "**Play** &, 2 **Play**, 3 &, 4 &, **Play** &, 2 **Play**, 3 &, 4 &, *etc.*"

Example 8

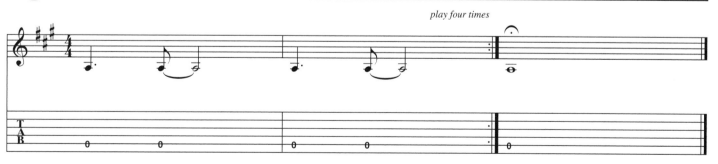

Practice these exercises steadily until you become comfortable with them. Once you feel that you've gotten used to playing these examples along with the backup track on the CD then you're ready to move along to the next section.

Part II: Scales and Arpeggios

In this section you'll be playing scales and arpeggios based on the rhythm exercises from *Part I*. As we had previously discussed, a *scale* is formed by notes moving up in a series of steps and an *arpeggio* is simply a chord that has been broken into single notes.

In addition, all of the exercises in this section should be played with a swing feel.

What does swing feel mean?
A *swing feel* means that you should play the example with a triplet feel. A *triplet* is when three notes share a beat or count equally. An *eighth-note triplet* is when three eighth notes share a quarter note or one beat. For example, count to yourself, "1 & a, 2 & a, 3 & a, 4 & a, *etc*."

So. . . what is swing feel?
Swing feel is when you play two eighth notes instead of three and give the first eighth note the value of the "1 &" count and the second eighth note the value of the "a" count.

Let's play some scales and arpeggios. . .

The following eight scales and arpeggios are to be played as whole notes and are not demonstrated on the CD. However, you should practice them with the backup track (CD Track 41). It is not only important to be able to play these scales and arpeggios, but also to be able to hear the differences between them.

A major

Our first scale is A major. Although A major is not a blues scale, it is very important to have a working understanding of this scale. The major scale is "the" standard scale and for that reason this is where we begin. The major scale is made up of scale degrees 1, 2, 3, 4, 5, 6, and 7. The A major scale is made up of the following notes: A, B, C♯, D, E, F♯, G♯, and A.

Example 9

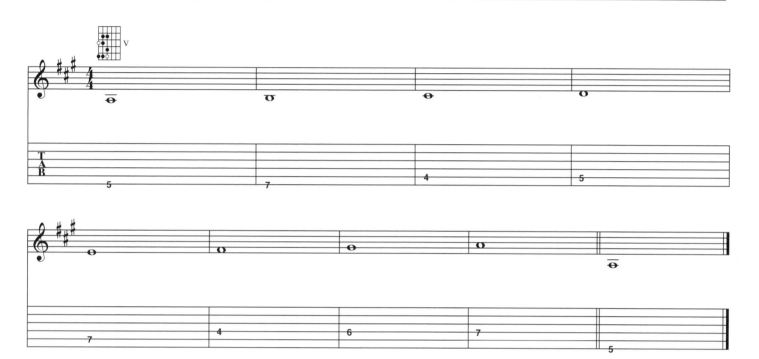

A Mixolydian

Mixolydian is simply a major scale with a ♭7 instead of a major 7. The only difference between A major and A Mixolydian is that the G♯ has been lowered to a G natural (in the Mixolydian scale). This gives A Mixolydian a dominant sound that works well against the dominant chords found in most blues progressions. The Mixolydian scale is made up of scale degrees 1, 2, 3, 4, 5, 6, and ♭7. The A Mixolydian scale is made up of the following notes: A, B, C♯, D, E, F♯, and G.

Example 10

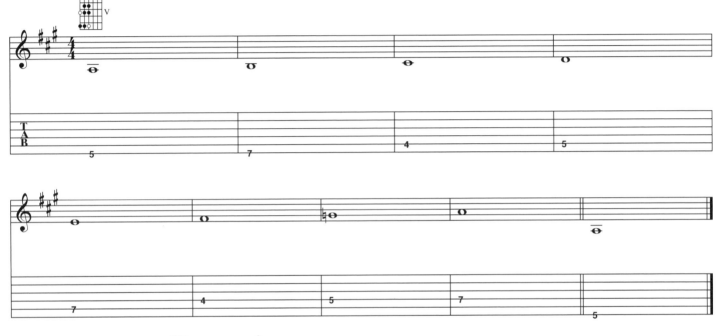

A7 arpeggio

The dominant 7 arpeggio is made up of the 1, 3, 5, and ♭7 scale degrees of the Mixolydian scale. A dominant 7 arpeggio and chord are both constructed from the same notes: A, C♯, E, and G.

Example 11

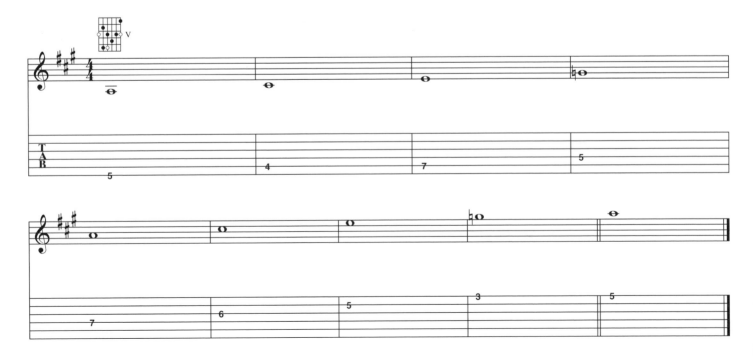

A pentatonic major scale

A pentatonic scale is made up of five notes or scale degrees. The scale degrees that make up this scale are 1, 2, 3, 5, and 6. The A pentatonic major scale is made up of the following notes: A, B, C♯, E, and F♯.

Example 12

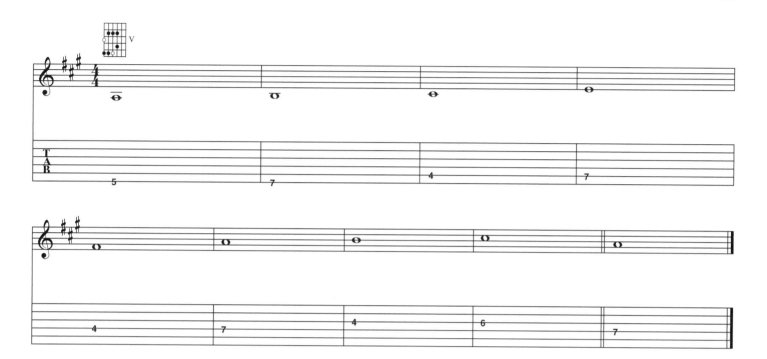

A pentatonic minor scale

This pentatonic scale contains scale degrees 1, ♭3, 4, 5, and ♭7. Notice that this scale falls nicely under your fingers to form a "box" pattern on the guitar's fretboard. The pentatonic minor scale is a *must* for any aspiring guitar player. This scale is made up of the following notes: A, C, D, E, and G.

Example 13

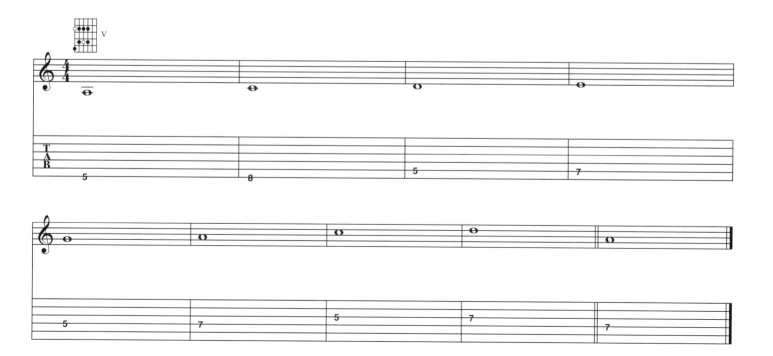

A pentatonic minor scale with added ♭5 note

We will refer to this scale as the pentatonic minor ♭5 scale from now on. As its name suggest it is a pentatonic minor scale with an added "blue note"—the ♭5. This scale is also sometimes referred to as the pentatonic blues. The A pentatonic minor scale with added ♭5 is made up of the following notes: A, C, D, E♭, E, and G.

Example 14

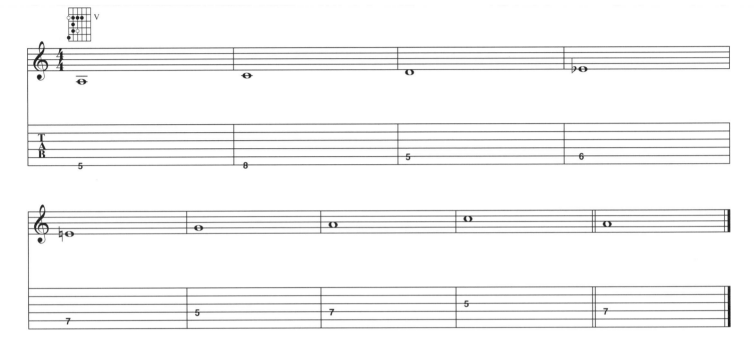

A blues scale with major 3 and ♭5 notes

We will refer to this scale as the blues scale from now on. The name of this scale says it all. The blues scale simply contains all of the good notes. It is made up of scale degrees 1, ♭3, 3, 4, ♭5, 5, and ♭7. The A blues scale is made up of the following notes: A, C, C♯, D, E♭, E, and G.

Example 15

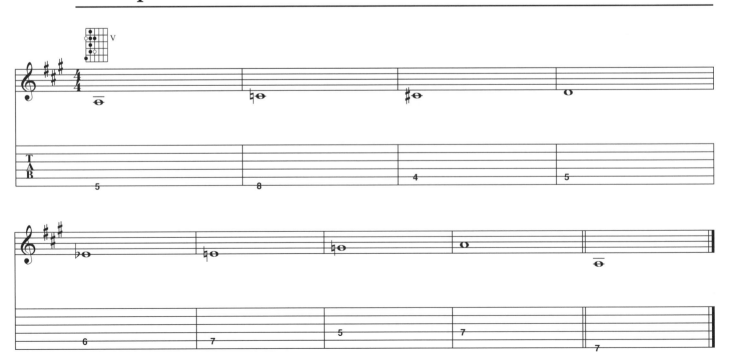

A7 arpeggio with added ♯9 and ♭5 notes

We'll refer to this arpeggio as an A7♯9♭5 from now on. The "blue notes" sound cool as you play the arpeggio from bottom to top. I've included this arpeggio as a reference. It's important to know where the "blue notes" are in relation to whatever scale or arpeggio that you're playing. The A7♯9♭5 arpeggio is made up of scale degrees 1, ♭3 (or ♯9), 3, ♭5, 5, and ♭7; and the following notes: A, C, C♯, E♭, E, and G.

Example 16

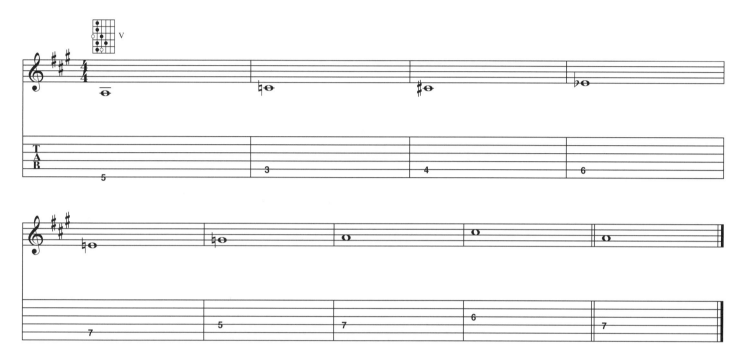

At this time you're probably asking, "What's a blue note?" Or, "What does a blue note mean?"

Blue notes are those notes (or scale degrees) that provide that blues sound to a scale, arpeggio, or chord. They are the notes that sound hip. The blue notes are scale degrees ♭3 (or ♯9), ♭5, and ♭7; or, in the key of A, notes C, E♭, and G.

Now, let's try playing them as half notes. . .

A major scale

14 **Example 17**

A Mixolydian

15 **Example 18**

A7 arpeggio

 16 # Example 19

A pentatonic major scale

17 # Example 20

A pentatonic minor scale

18 Example 21

A pentatonic minor ♭5 scale

19 Example 22

A blues scale

20 Example 23

A7♯9♭5 arpeggio

21 Example 24

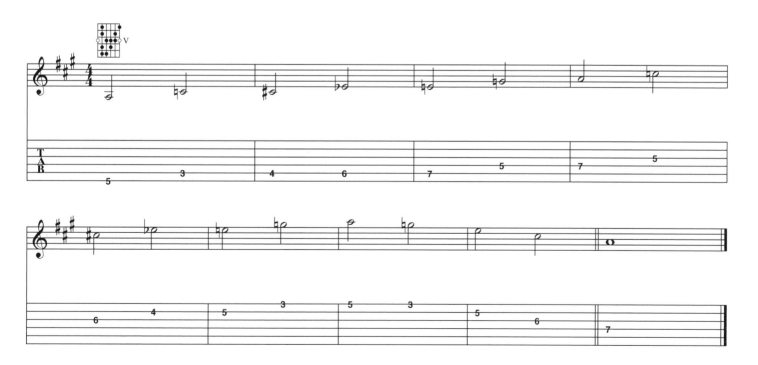

And now, let's try playing them as quarter notes. . .

A major scale

22 **Example 25**

A Mixolydian

23 **Example 26**

A7 arpeggio

24 **Example 27**

A pentatonic major scale

25 **Example 28**

A pentatonic minor scale

26 **Example 29**

A pentatonic minor ♭5 scale

27 **Example 30**

A blues scale

28 Example 31

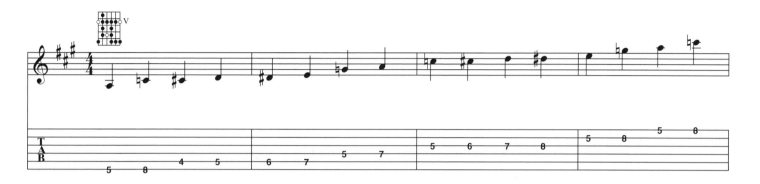

A7♯9♭5 arpeggio

29 Example 32

And finally, let's try playing them as eighth notes. . .

A major scale

30 Example 33

A Mixolydian

31 Example 34

A7 arpeggio

32 Example 35

A pentatonic major scale

33 Example 36

A pentatonic minor scale

34 Example 37

A pentatonic minor ♭5 scale

35 Example 38

A blues scale

36 Example 39

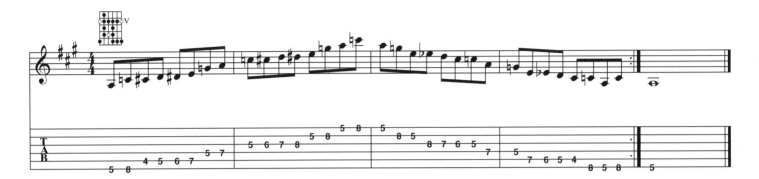

A7♯9♭5 arpeggio

37 Example 40

Picking Exercises

The following examples will demonstrate some suggestions for practicing the scales and arpeggios in this book as well as any new scales and arpeggios that you happen to discover. The examples for the A major scale are included on the CD.

Eighth-Note Picking Exercise

Each note gets played twice once with a downstroke and once with an upstroke. This is *alternate picking*. Practicing scales in this fashion will help develop picking technique and rhythmic control. Musicians refer to this as "chops."

38 **Example 41**

Eighth-Note Triplet Picking Exercise

This example will teach you more about control and help you to "feel" the swing that we discussed earlier. Continue to use alternate picking, "down-up-down, up-down-up, *etc.*" The pick strokes will even out in the end.

39 ## Example 42

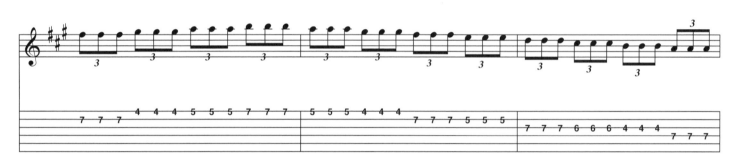

Sixteenth-Note Picking Exercise

This one is a little tricky. Four pick strokes per beat against a swing feel. "Down-up-down-up, down-up-down-up, *etc*." Keep your picking hand loose and listen to the groove. It is very important to play these exercises "in time." It's more important to be able to play "in the pocket" than to be able to play as fast as possible.

Example 43

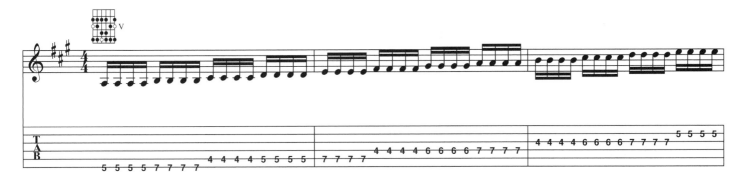

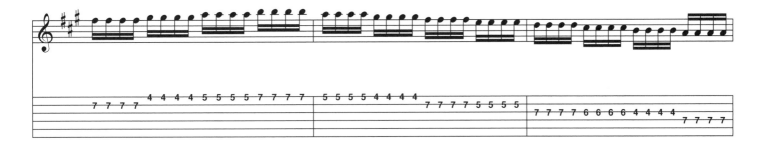

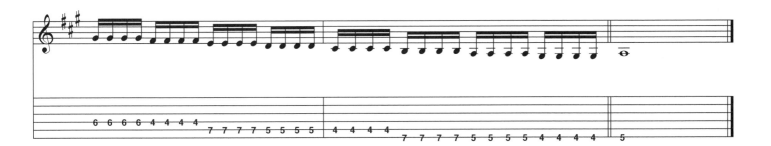

The following picking examples have been written out for your consideration. Practice them with CD Track 41.

A Mixolydian

Example 44

Example 45

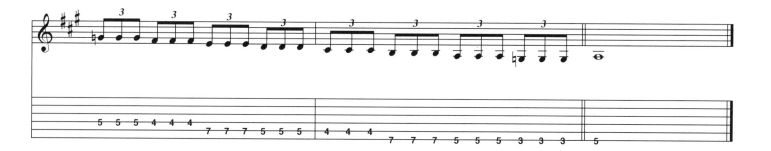

Example 46

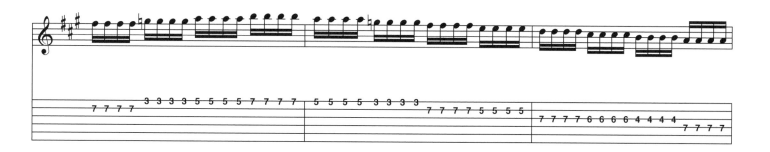

38

A7 arpeggio

Example 47

Example 48

Example 49

A pentatonic major scale

Example 50

Example 51

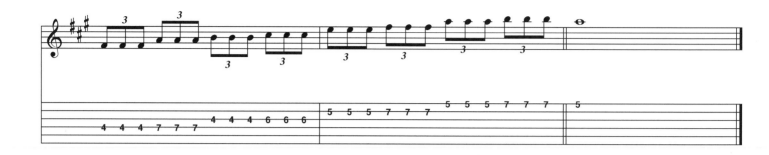

Example 52

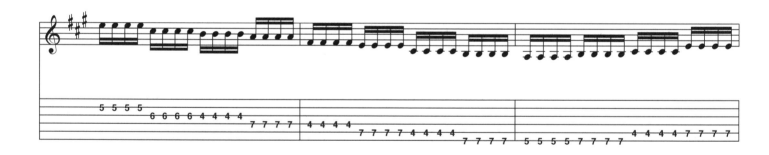

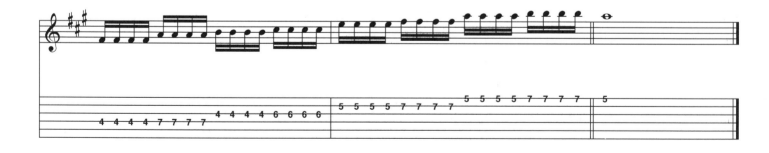

A pentatonic minor scale

Example 53

Example 54

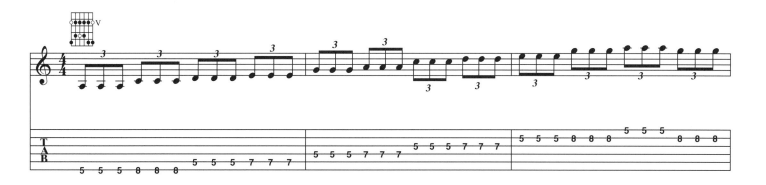

Example 55

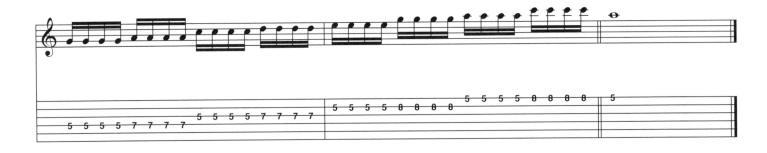

A pentatonic minor ♭5 scale

Example 56

Example 57

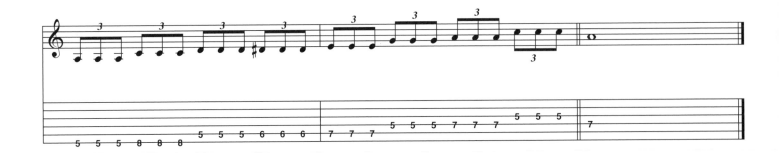

Example 58

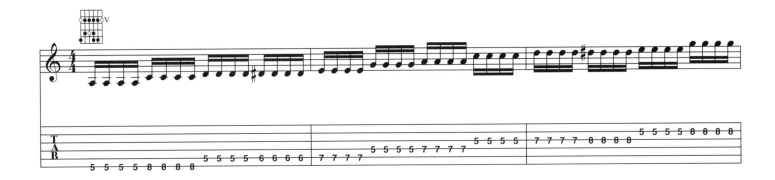

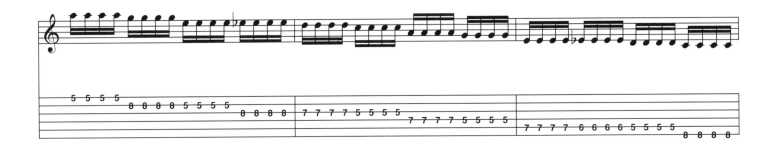

A blues scale

Example 59

Example 60

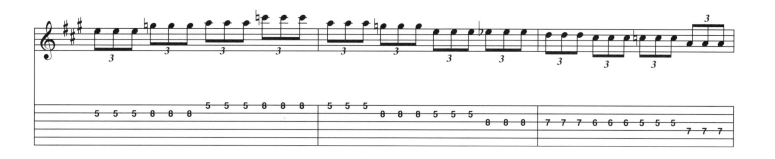

Example 61

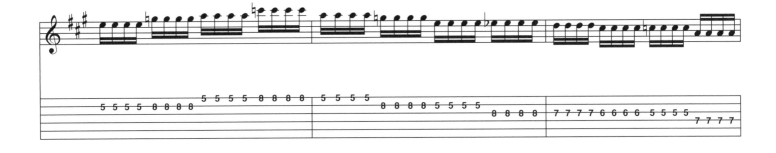

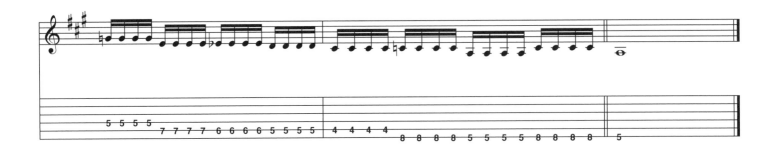

A7♯9♭5 arpeggio

Example 62

Example 63

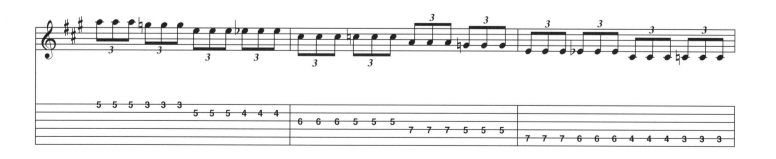

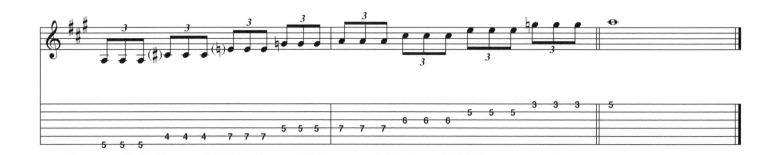

Example 64

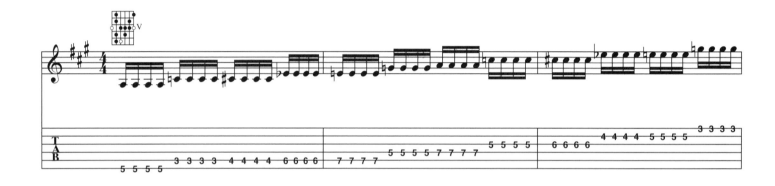

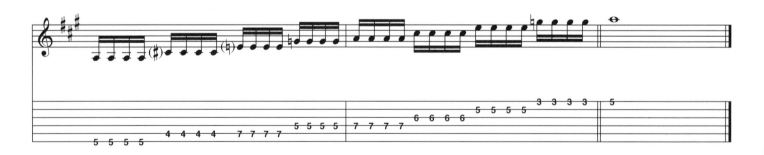

At this point you've probably been practicing a lot. But the payoff is starting to show. You should now have all of the scales and arpeggios memorized, and have the ability to play them comfortably with the backup track. We're now ready to move on. . .

Part III: Playing Over Chord Changes

The key to playing or improvising solos is simply to be aware of what's ahead. Knowing the chord changes helps but it's not enough. Hearing the changes as they happen is what we're after. Up till now we've been playing scales and arpeggios over a one-chord rhythm pattern. At the same time, we've been training our fingers to play scales and arpeggios over this one-chord rhythm pattern. In addition, we've been training our ears to hear the differences between each scale and arpeggio. We're now ready to apply what we've been learning to playing over chord changes.

The first part of this section is going to be played over a I to IV chord progression. What this means is that, in the key of A, the A is the I chord and the D is the IV chord. The examples are sixteen measures in length starting with an A (or I) chord for four bars, going to a D (or IV) chord for four bars, back to the A chord for four bars, and then again to the D chord for four bars, finally ending on an A chord.

A picture is worth a thousand words. Check out the chord chart below.

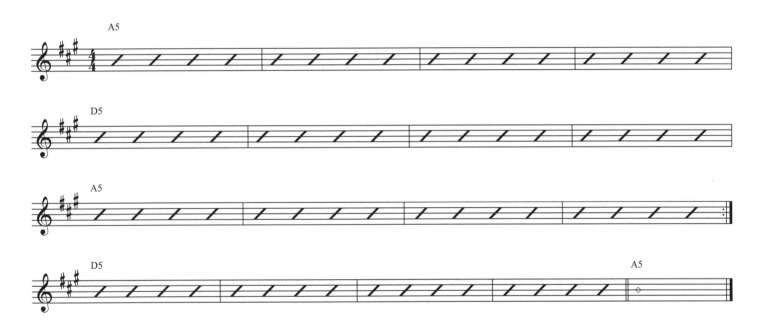

The idea is to move the scales and arpeggios over each chord as it changes. For example, A scales and arpeggios are played over the A chord and D scales and arpeggios are played over the D chord. We're basically treating each chord as the key of the moment. When the chord changes, so do the scales and arpeggios.

First, try playing the scales and arpeggios as quarter notes. If this proves too difficult for the moment then try half notes.

I–IV major scale

43 **Example 65**

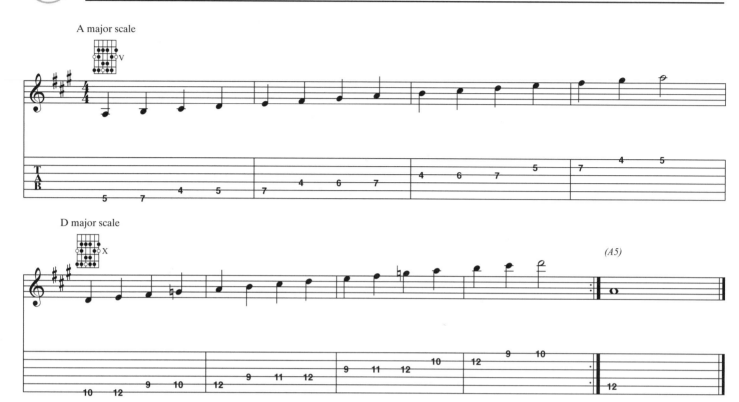

Once you get the hang of it you can move on to eighth notes.

I–IV major scale

44 **Example 66**

Now try this with the other scales and arpeggios.

I–IV Mixolydian

 Example 67

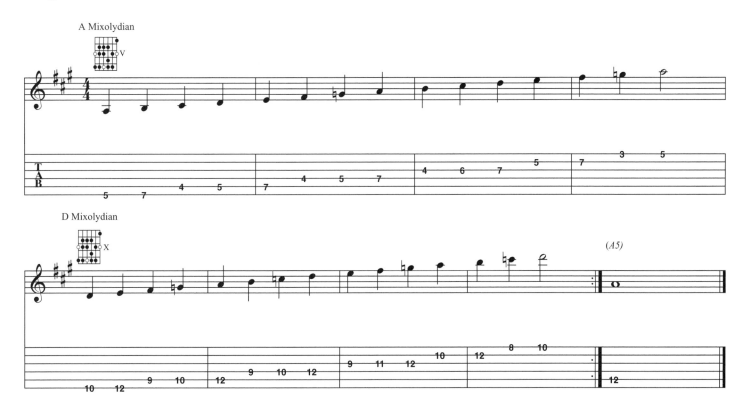

 Example 68

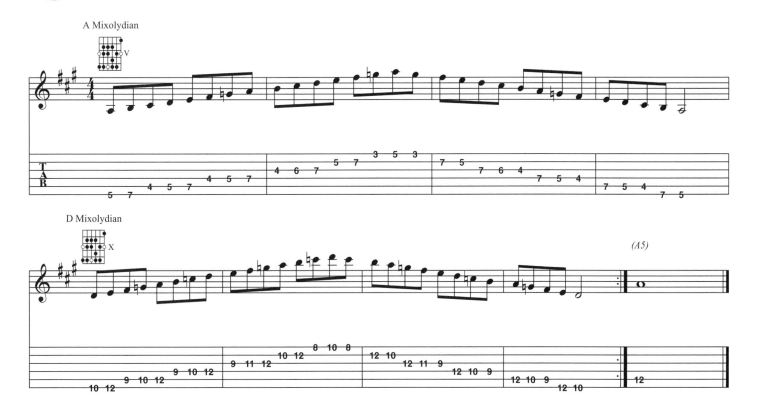

I–IV 7 arpeggio

47 # Example 69

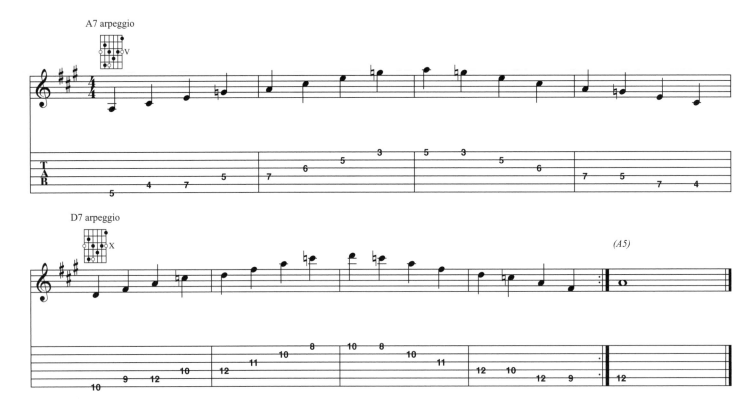

48 # Example 70

I–IV pentatonic major scale

 ## Example 71

Example 72

I–IV pentatonic minor scale

 51 Example 73

A pentatonic minor

D pentatonic minor

52 Example 74

A pentatonic minor

D pentatonic minor

I–IV pentatonic minor ♭5 scale

Example 75

A pentatonic minor add ♭5

D pentatonic minor add ♭5

(A5)

Example 76

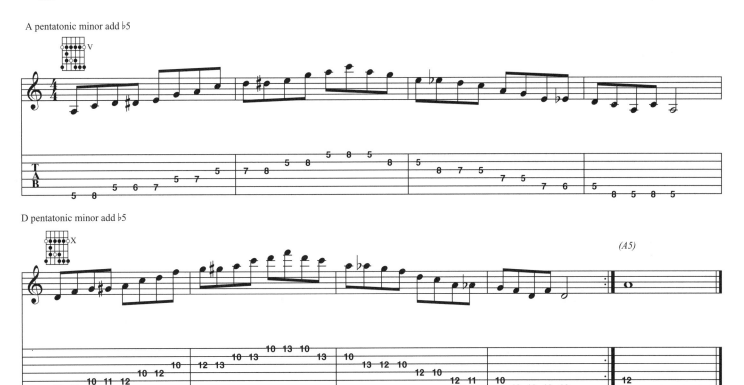

A pentatonic minor add ♭5

D pentatonic minor add ♭5

(A5)

I–IV blues scale

55 Example 77

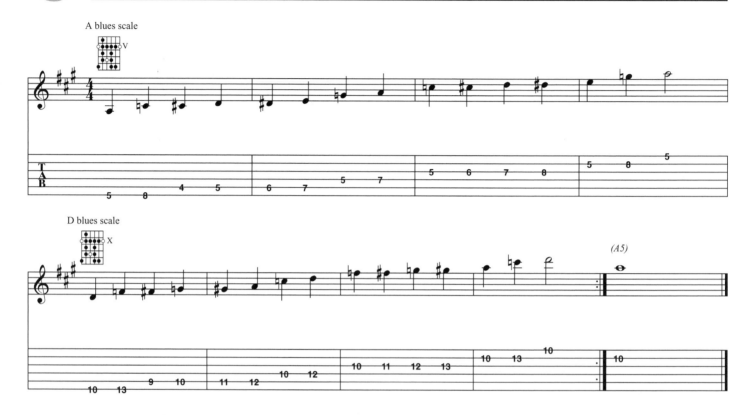

56 Example 78

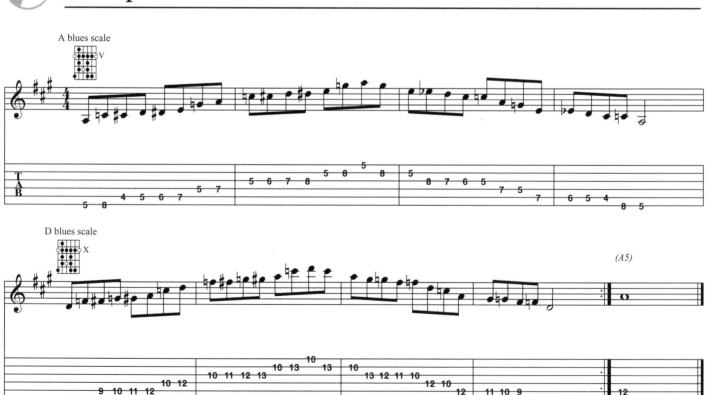

I–IV 7♯9♭5 arpeggio

57 Example 79

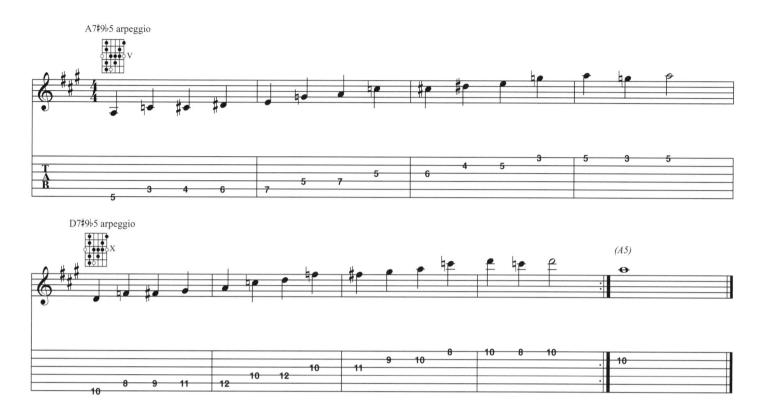

58 Example 80

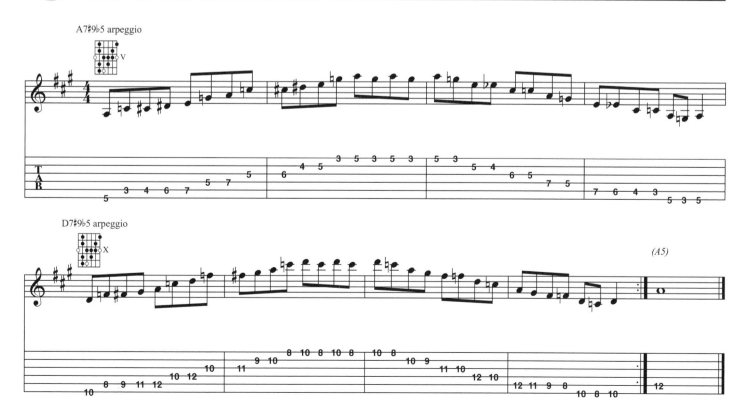

The second part of this section is going to be played over a I–IV–V chord progression. What this means is that, in the key of A, the A is the I chord, D is the IV chord, and E is the V chord. These examples are also sixteen measures in length starting with an A (or I) chord for four bars, going to a D (or IV) chord for four bars, then to the E (or V) chord for four bars, and finally back to an A chord for four bars and out.

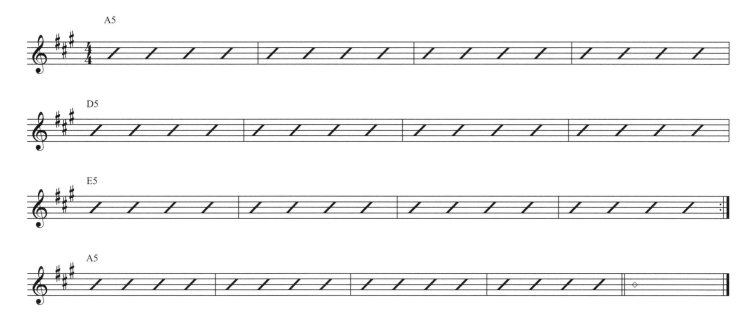

The following I–IV–V progression examples are demonstrated with eighth notes. Again, if this proves too difficult try playing these exercises using half or quarter notes.

I–IV–V major scale

60 Example 81

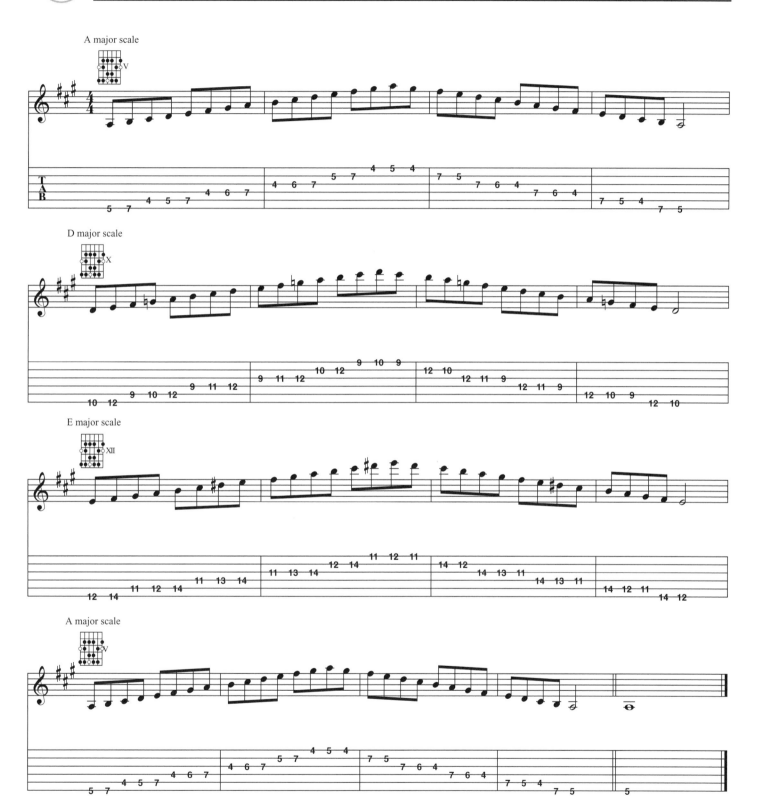

I–IV–V Mixolydian

61 **Example 82**

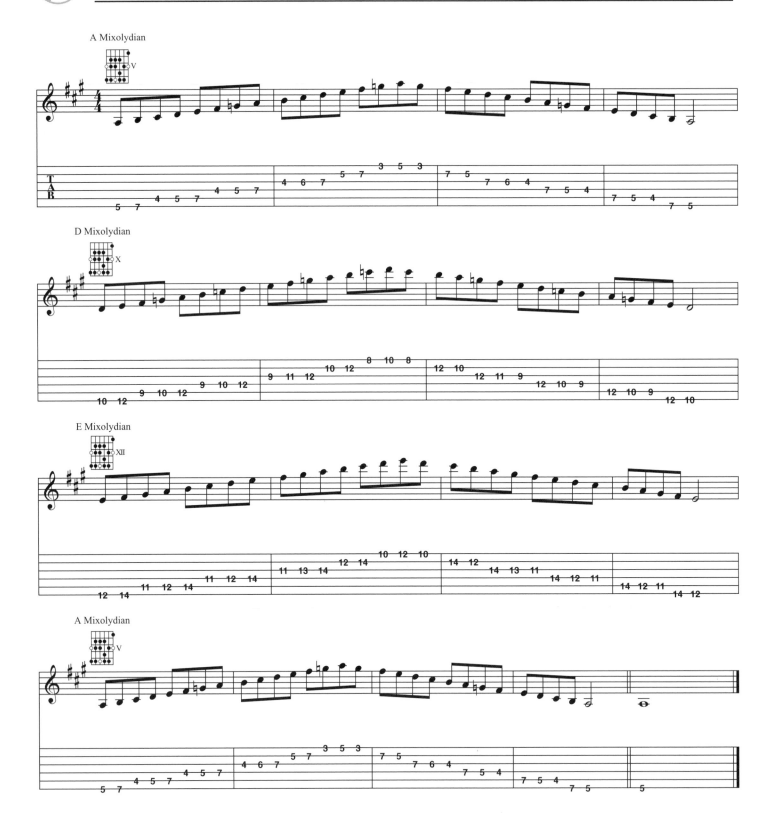

I–IV–V 7 arpeggio

62 ## Example 83

I–IV–V pentatonic major scale

63 Example 84

I–IV–V pentatonic minor scale

64 Example 85

I–IV–V pentatonic minor ♭5 scale

Example 86

I–IV–V blues scale

Example 87

I–IV–V 7♯9♭5 arpeggio

 67 # Example 88

 68 Now that you understand the concept of playing over changes, you can take a lick or a riff and practice moving it over the chords on the backup tracks. *The Gig Bag Book of Practical Pentatonics* (AM 948805), published by Amsco, contains over 540 licks and riffs. You could also use examples from various guitar magazines or transcriptions that are available.

Remember, this is only the beginning.

69 # Part IV: Intros, Turnarounds, and Endings

Turnarounds occur at the end of a section (usually the last two measures) and bring you into the next section. As its name implies, a turnaround riff adds motion and turns around or leads into the next verse, chorus, or bridge.

Endings are self-explanatory and indicate the completion of a song.

In this section both turnarounds and endings are demonstrated in the same example. The first two measures are the turnaround and the third or last measure is the ending.

The following exercises show you ten different ways of playing turnarounds and endings for the same song. Try experimenting by mixing and matching measures from the different examples to create your own turnaround riffs.

70 ## Example 89

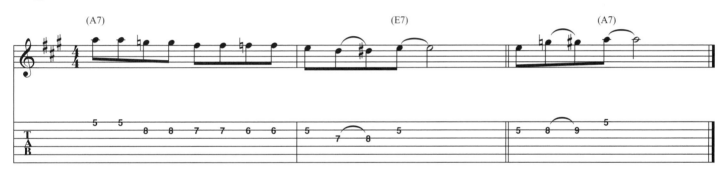

71 ## Example 90

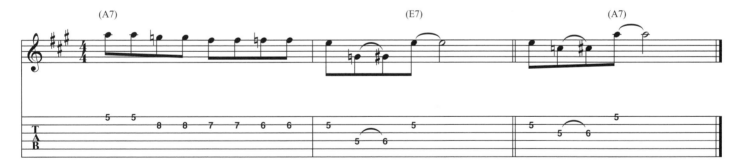

72 ## Example 91

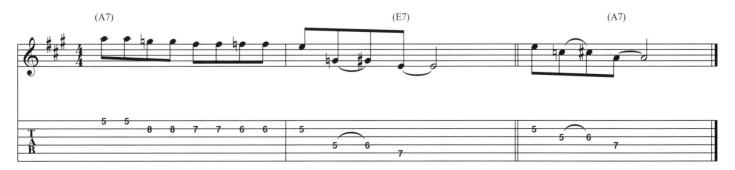

73 Example 92

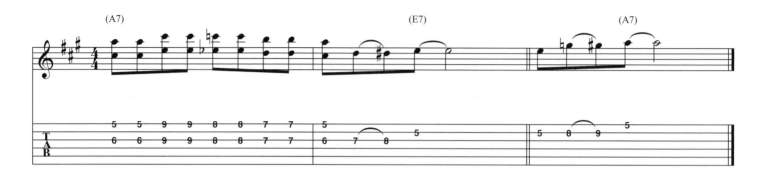

74 Example 93

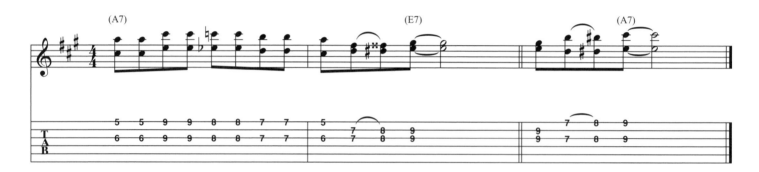

75 Example 94

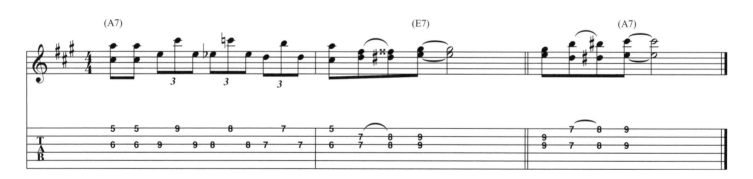

76 Example 95

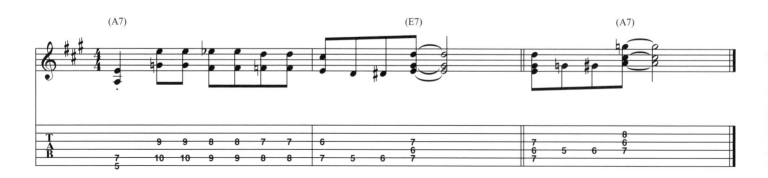

Example 96

 Example 97

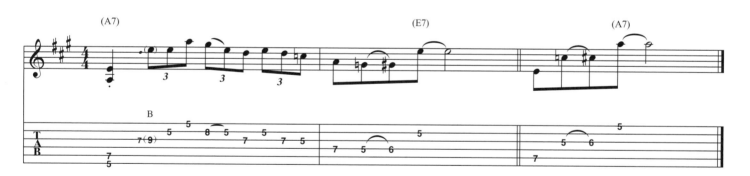 Example 98

You can also substitute the last measure with the second measure for a more abrupt ending. These combination turnaround/ending riffs are usually discussed beforehand; however, more advanced players can "improvise" these ending riffs with subtle eye contact or, if possible, hand gestures.

Once you memorize these riffs you can recall them in a live playing situation with confidence.

Part V: How to Create a Solo

Let's take a look at what we've learned so far:
- Rhythms and Rests
- Scales and Arpeggios
- Playing over Chord Changes
- Intros, Turnarounds, and Endings

In this section we're going to discuss improvisational techniques that will help you to develop your own solos. Each of the five solos below demonstrates a different technique or concept played over a traditional 12-bar blues progression.

Take a look at the chart below and notice the repeat at the second to last measure.

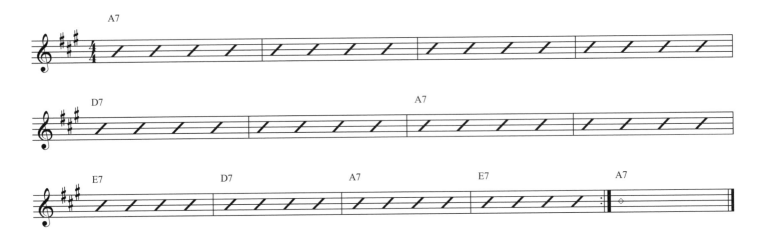

Guide Tone Ex. 1

A *guide tone* is the most important note in a chord. In Part III we learned how to move scales and arpeggios over chords. Guide tone movement is subtle and more effective. The guide tones in a dominant 7 chord are the 3 and ♭7 scale degrees. The 1 and 5 are not as important. So in a I–IV–V progression the guide tones can indicate the chord movement by only moving a half step in either direction. For example, the guide tones for A7 are C♯ and G, for D7 are F♯ and C, and for E7 are G♯ and D. By moving between the C, C♯, and D you can outline the chord movement using the chord's "inner voices." Listen to the first verse of the following example for a demonstration of this concept.

The second verse illustrates the 3 and ♭7 of each chord played as half notes. Notice that you can hear the "color" or quality of each chord just by playing the guide tones.

Example 99

Guide Tone Ex. 2

This next solo demonstrates the same concept that was discussed in the previous example. Check out the first verse. Notice the change in rhythm from the second verse of the previous example. We're still playing the same two notes but by changing the rhythm the phrase sounds more lyrical. Also, notice the *slide* into the first note of each measure. (A slide is executed by picking a note one fret below the intended note and quickly "sliding up" to the intended note.)

The second verse begins with a slide into the first note as before. The notes following the two guide tones are from the A Mixolydian scale. Notice the blue note on beat three in the first measure of the second verse. The minor third (C) hammers on to the major third (C♯) providing this phrase with a bluesy flavor. (A *hammeron* is played by picking a note and then "hammering on" to a higher note with a finger from your fret hand.) The phrase is then repeated and followed by a variation in bars three and four of the second verse. We then change the guide tones over the D7 chord and that phrase is followed by the variation. At the E7 chord, we simply play the same phrase that we played over the D7 chord except that we transpose it up two frets (or a whole step). Also, note that the last note over the A7 chord is a D eighth note that is tied to a D whole note in the final measure of the second verse. The D is the ♭7 scale degree of the E7 chord. This note occurs before the chord is actually played. This is called an *anticipation*. We then end on the C♯, scale degree 3 of the A7 chord.

This solo has it all. The guide tone theme is established in the first verse, developed in the first two measures of the second verse, and played with a variation in measures three and four of the second verse. Along the way the following techniques were also discussed: slides, hammerons, and anticipations.

 Example 100

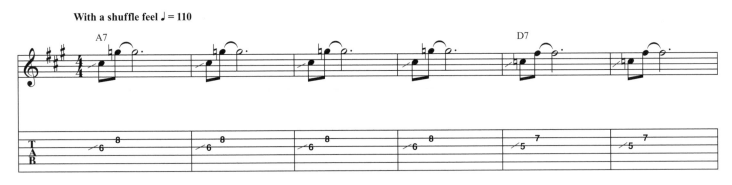

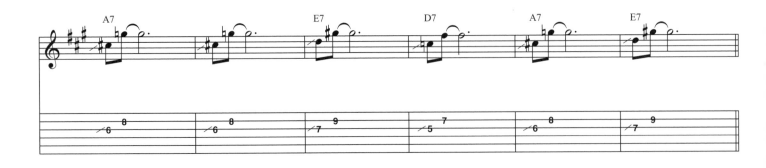

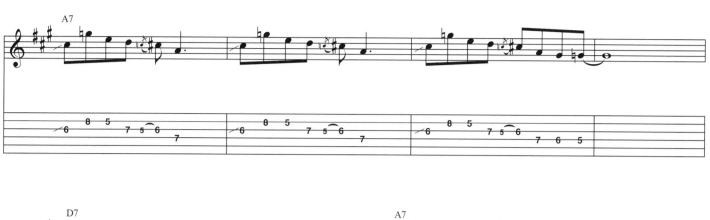

Notice that we're starting to sound more musical. This solo was played in a five-fret region of the guitar's fretboard and we were able to outline the underlying chord changes. You don't have to "skate" all over the neck to sound good.

Bends and Hammerons

This solo is based on the minor pentatonic scale and demonstrates two techniques: bends and hammerons. The first verse is played with a simple two-bar phrase that is centered around the bend. The bend in this case is a whole-step bend. It is important to bend the string to the proper pitch as a poorly executed bend is the same as playing a wrong note. Notice that we move the phrase around the I, IV, and V chords as we did in Part III.

In the second verse, the bend is followed by a hammeron from the minor to the major third. Also, check out the hammerons played during the last two measures of the tune. Rather than resolving to the root below, we resolve the hammeron to the root an octave above. This is called *octave displacement*.

 Example 101

Hammerons and Pulloffs

A *descending eighth-note triplet run* is featured in this solo. The first verse is played with a pentatonic major scale and the second verse is played with a pentatonic minor scale.

This example also combines hammerons and pulloffs. A *pulloff* is played by "pulling off" with a finger from your fret hand to a lower note. In this example the hammerons and pulloffs are executed with one stroke of the pick. For example, in the first measure, pick the first note A and then hammer on to the B note two frets above and pull off back to the A. These three notes are played as an eighth-note triplet and repeated similarly on the adjacent strings. And there you have a descending eighth-note triplet run.

85 # Example 102

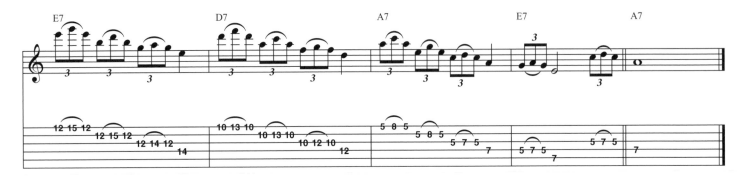

Doublestops

Doublestops are executed by playing two notes at the same time. This technique was made popular by the lead-playing style of Chuck Berry. The first verse demonstrates a doublestop phrase and the use of guide tone movement over the D7 and E7 chords.

The second verse uses the same phrase with a more complex rhythm pattern. Remember to relax as you play the eighth-note triplet doublestops. The second verse is reminiscent of slide-guitar master Elmore James.

86 # Example 103

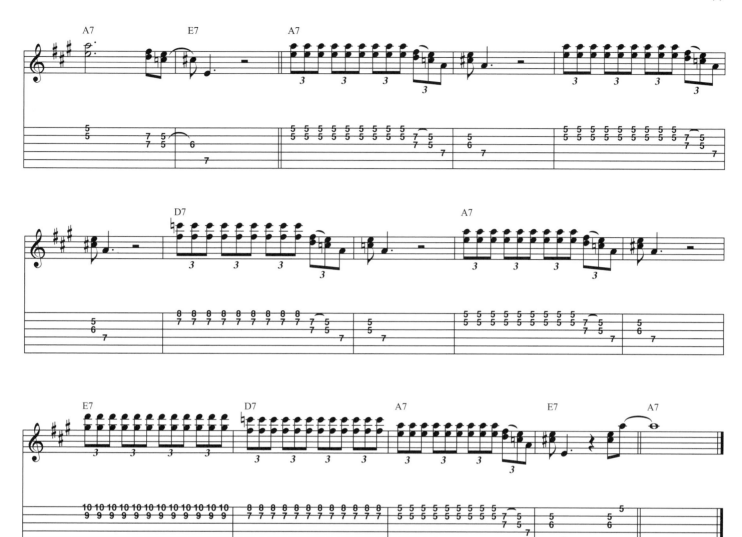

Let's review the techniques discussed in this section:
- Guide Tones
- Slides
- Hammerons and Pulloffs
- Bending
- Anticipation
- Octave Displacement
- Descending Runs
- Doublestops

These improvisational techniques when used with the scales and arpeggios from Part II will provide you with a solid foundation for blues lead guitar playing. You should now understand the basic concepts behind creating a solo.

The following five solos include some different chord progressions and rhythmic feels. Minor, Latin, Slow, Jazz, and Rock styles are demonstrated using 12-bar and 8-bar progressions. There is a chord chart prior to the transcription for your consideration.

Minor Latin Blues

Let's face it, Latin rhythms are contagious. Many great blues artists have enjoyed playing with a Latin-style groove. West-side Chicago's Otis Rush and the ever popular B.B. King used Latin rhythms in their music. Jazz legends Wes Montgomery and Kenny Burrell recorded minor Latin blues tunes as well.

This tune is a traditional 12-bar blues played with minor chords over a Latin rhythm. The *motif* or main musical phrase is based on chord tones followed by a minor pentatonic riff. The second verse is played with a variation on the minor pentatonic riff. This variation is based on the bending riff in Ex. 101. You don't need to change much to create interest.

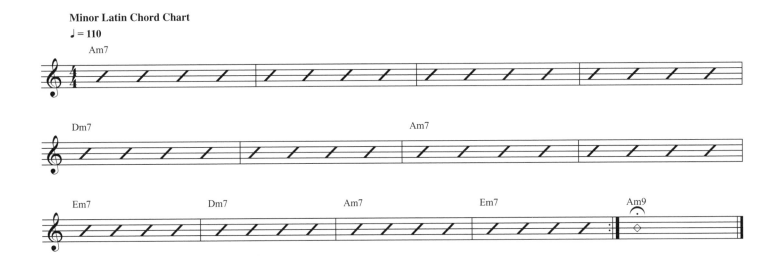

Minor Latin Blues

Slow 8-Bar Blues

When Jimi Hendrix was paying his dues, playing the chitlin circuit, he performed with many Rhythm and Blues acts. This slow 8-bar blues is similar to the popular R&B ballads of the day.

To begin with, this tune has a triplet feel to it. Notice that the time signature is in 12 rather than 4. However, the count off is still in four. Secondly, the solo begins with pick-up notes. *Pick-up notes* are those notes played before the first measure. Also check out the E+ chord played during the pick-up measure. This is common practice in this style of blues playing. And finally, the motif is based on an A pentatonic major while the descending melody line (during the second half of the first verse) is based on notes from the A Mixolydian scale. The second verse has an ascending melody line during the beginning half of the section. Descending and ascending melodies is yet another method used for creating interest.

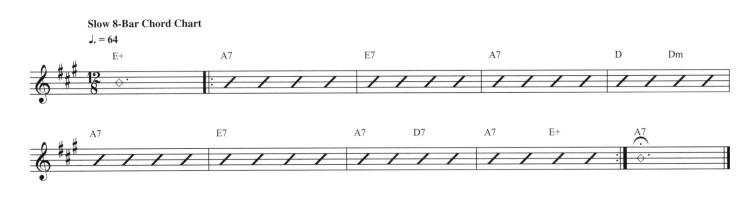

91 92 Slow 8-Bar Blues

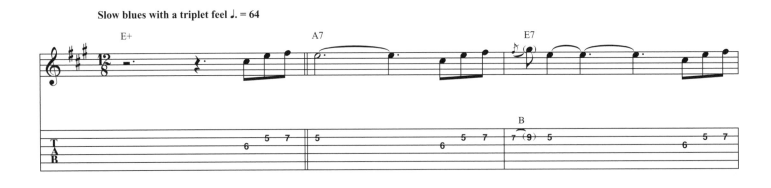

Jazz Blues

Horn or swing bands usually have a more sophisticated (or uptown) sound. This is reflect-ed in their choice of harmony. "Jazz Blues" is a traditional 12-bar blues with chord substi-tutions. Playing over these changes can be a lot of fun, so don't be intimidated by all of the chords. The simple motif in the first verse is a three-note minor pentatonic riff. That's it!

The second verse demonstrates the *call-and-response* technique. The motif has not changed but is answered first by a simple D7 arpeggio in the second measure. The motif is then repeated and answered by the A blues scale in the fourth measure. Once again, the motif is repeated but this time is answered by a D♯°7 arpeggio (this arpeggio sounds cool over any D7 chord). Motif and A blues scale again, followed by the motif and an E7 arpeggio, finishing up with motif, blues scale, and motif.

93 94 Jazz Blues

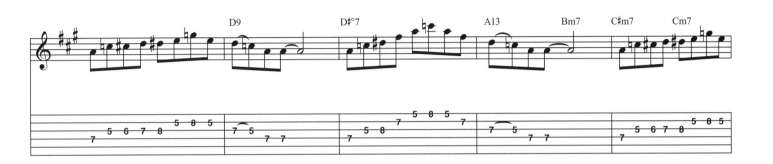

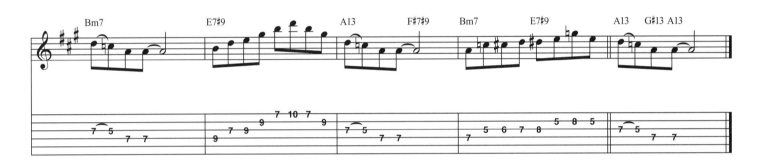

8-Bar Rock Blues

This tune begins with pick-up notes and a doublestop phrase. The pick-up note lick is repeated every four bars throughout this tune. This creates a feeling of continuity throughout the solo as opposed to chaining together a bunch of meaningless riffs that don't make any sense. Notice the motif in the second measure over an E7 chord. This motif is repeated four bars later over another E7 chord in the sixth measure. Also check out the D7 arpeggio in measure three. (If you're feeling adventurous, try playing the D♯°7 arpeggio from the previous tune.) Finally, check out the last two measures. This is the same turnaround riff found in Ex. 97.

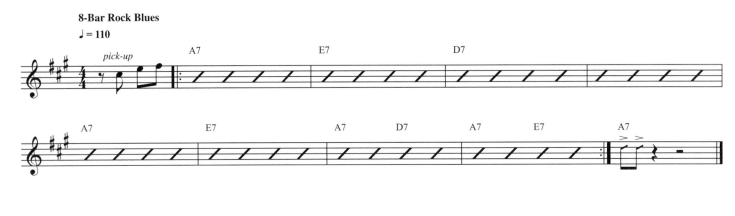

8-Bar Rock Blues

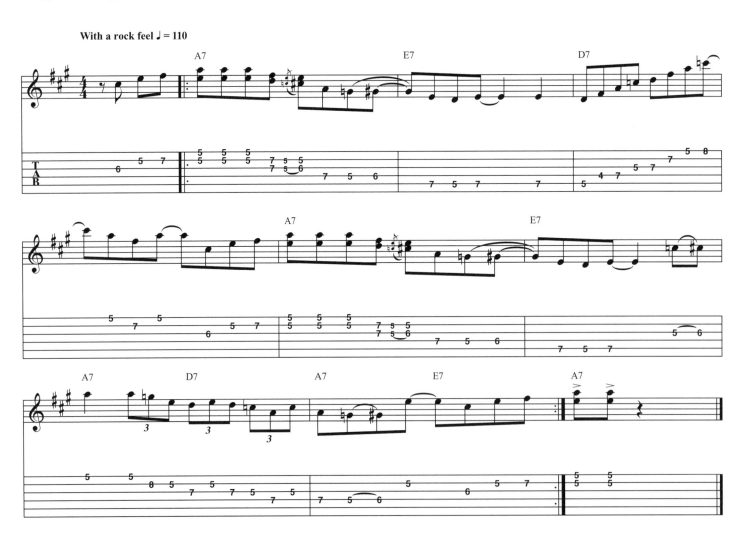

Black Magic Blues

This last tune is a 'tip of the hat' to blues-rock legend Carlos Santana. This minor blues progression brings to mind Santana's cover of the Peter Green classic "Black Magic Woman." Bends, guide tones, bend-and-release riffs, and anticipations are found throughout this solo. Notice the descending bend-and-release riffs in the last four bars of the first verse.

The second verse is the same as the first with the exception that it is played up an octave. Instead of playing at the fifth fret position you'll be playing the same solo at the seventeenth fret position. This creates a feeling of excitement during the second verse.

Black Magic Blues Chord Chart

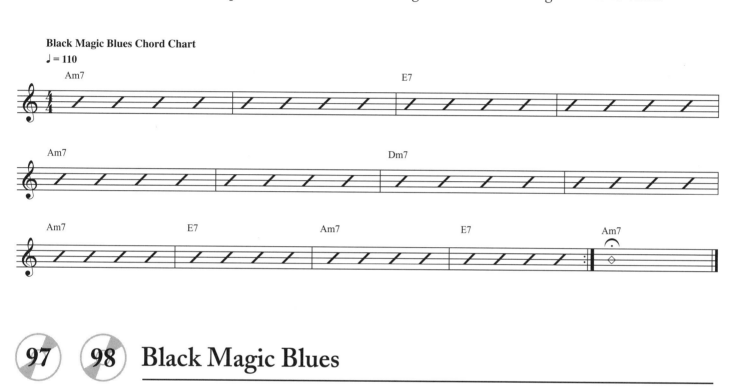

Black Magic Blues

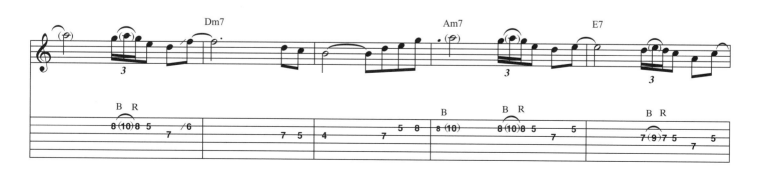

(99) In Conclusion

Congratulations! You should now have a solid foundation for playing blues lead guitar. At this time you should seek out other players who share the same interest in the blues and jam with them, learn from them, and ultimately, become one of them. Find out what blues standards are popular with the local blues players in your area and learn them.

The greatest teachers are the players that you idolize—Stevie Ray Vaughan once said of B.B. King's album *Live at the Regal*, "I go back to that record and it's like a little book. . . there's always something new," and of his record collection, ". . . they're all little books." So take Stevie Ray's advice and listen to as many recordings of your favorite players as possible. Learn the blues straight from the source. Good Luck!

"When you're playing and all of a sudden you realize your toes are just tightened up and you get a chill all the way up your back because of what you just gave somebody and what they gave back to you. That's probably the biggest thrill. Or, you're playing someplace and you just hit a note and people start screaming—that's it. You gave them a thrill, or you soothed them. That's what the blues do to me."
–Stevie Ray Vaughan